Focusing 2 Finish

21 Day Inspirational Affirmations

Printed in United States of America

Copyright © 2024 Cassandra Ewings-Moye

ISBN: 9798879817096

All rights reserved. Without limiting the rights under the copyright reserved above, no part of this publication may be reproduced, stored in, or introduced into a retrieval system, or transmitted in any form or by any means (electronic, mechanical, photocopying, recording, or otherwise) without prior written permission.

Table of Contents

Focusing 2 Finish 1

21-Day Affirmations 1

Chapter 1: Meet the Author - Cassandra Ewings-Moye: A Life Transformed 2

Chapter 2: The Power of Affirmations - How Words Shape Our Lives 4

Chapter 3: The 21-Day Affirmation Challenge - Your Path to Personal Transformation 5

Conclusion: Your Journey to Greatness 20

Focusing 2 Finish
21-Day Affirmations

It's easy to lose sight of our true purpose in the hustle and bustle of our daily lives. We often find ourselves stuck in a cycle of negative thoughts, self-doubt, and unfulfilled dreams. But what if I told you that you have the power to change your life and become the best version of yourself?

Focusing 2 Finish: 21-Day Affirmations is a roadmap to self-realization designed to nurture your spirit and awaken your inner strength. Every spoken word carries energy that influences our journey. You'll navigate a path of self-love, resilience, and purposeful living through powerful declarations, insightful explanations, relatable anecdotes, and practical exercises. Throughout these pages, you will transform your mindset, learn to harness the power of positive statements, and be well on your way to fulfilling your purpose with passion and conviction.

Chapter 1

Meet the Author - Cassandra Ewings-Moye

A Life Transformed

Cassandra Ewings-Moye is an inspirational author whose life story serves as a testament to the fact that no matter where you come from or what challenges you face, you can rise above them and embrace your divine calling. Born into a world of challenges, Cassandra's life could have quickly taken a different path. However, her unwavering faith in God and her unshakable determination to become the best version of herself propelled her forward.

As she navigated life's twists and turns, Cassandra's calling became increasingly apparent. She became a beloved media personality, using her platform to inspire, empower, and uplift others. Through her experiences, she realized the profound impact of words and the importance of speaking life into existence. Driven by her deep love for God and determination to finish strong, Cassandra created this powerful guide to be a wellspring of hope and inspiration for you on your journey toward greatness.

Chapter 2

The Power of Affirmations - How Words Shape Our Lives

Words are powerful tools that shape our thoughts, emotions, and actions. They can elevate, encourage, motivate, or drag us down into self-doubt. Think about the last time someone said something encouraging or uplifting to you. How did it make you feel? Chances are, those words positively impacted your mood, self-esteem, and motivation. Now, recall a time when you heard negative or discouraging words. How did they affect you? Negative words can erode our confidence, hinder our progress, and even lead to self-sabotage.

It's not just the words spoken by others that matter; the words we say to ourselves are equally powerful. Our internal dialogue shapes our self-perception and beliefs, ultimately influencing our actions and decisions. Daily affirmations harness the incredible power of words, shaping our reality and guiding us to become our best selves.

Chapter 3

The 21-Day Affirmation Challenge - Your Path to Personal Transformation

---

Now that you understand the power of affirmations, it's time to embark on your 21-day affirmation challenge. Each day is an opportunity to strengthen your faith, transform your mindset, and embrace your unique purpose.

Day 1: Created

- **Affirmation:** "I am created with purpose and intention. My existence has meaning and value."
- **Explanation:** Your existence is not accidental; you were created with a specific purpose in mind. This affirmation invites you to embrace the idea that you are a unique and valuable part of the universe.
- **Anecdote:** Imagine a skilled artist crafting a masterpiece. Each brushstroke is deliberate, and each color is carefully chosen. You are that

masterpiece; your creator has invested great care in shaping who you are.

- **Exercise:** Spend some time today reflecting on your life journey. What moments have brought you joy or fulfillment? These could be clues to your purpose. Write down your thoughts and feelings.

Day 2: Called

- **Affirmation:** "I am called to a unique purpose. I embrace my calling with enthusiasm and dedication."
- **Explanation:** You have a calling that sets you apart from others. Embracing this calling with enthusiasm and dedication can lead to a more meaningful and fulfilling life.
- **Anecdote:** Consider famous figures like Martin Luther King Jr. or Mother Teresa. They were called to make a profound impact on the world. Your calling may not be on that scale, but it's equally important in the grand scheme of things.
- **Exercise:** Write a letter to yourself describing your calling and the impact you hope to make. Keep this letter as a source of inspiration throughout your journey.

Day 3: Chosen

- **Affirmation:** "I am chosen for a great purpose. I accept the responsibility and honor of my divine calling."
- **Explanation:** You are not only created and called; you are chosen. Embracing this affirmation means recognizing the unique qualities and gifts that make you the ideal person to fulfill your purpose.
- **Anecdote:** Think of yourself as a puzzle piece that perfectly fits into the grand puzzle of life. Without you, the picture is incomplete. You are chosen to complete it.
- **Exercise:** List your strengths, talents, and unique qualities. How do these attributes align with your sense of purpose? Reflect on how your uniqueness makes you ideal for your calling.

Day 4: Accountability: The New Journey

- **Affirmation:** "I am accountable for my journey. I take ownership of my actions and decisions."
- **Explanation:** Accountability is the foundation of personal growth. This affirmation encourages you to take responsibility for your choices and actions, recognizing that they shape your journey.

- **Anecdote:** Consider a GPS navigation system; it can guide you, but you have to decide where you want to go and follow its directions. Similarly, you are responsible for steering your life journey.
- **Exercise:** Take a moment to journal about a past situation where you took full accountability for your actions. What did you learn from that experience? How can you apply those lessons to your current journey?

Day 5: Pure Intentions-GREATNESS
- **Affirmation:** "My intentions are pure and aligned with greatness. I attract positive outcomes through my intentions."
- **Explanation:** Your intentions shape your reality. You invite positive outcomes into your life by aligning them with greatness and purity.
- **Anecdote:** Think of intentions as seeds you plant in the soil of your mind. The quality of those seeds determines the quality of the harvest. Purity ensures a bountiful yield.
- **Exercise:** Choose an intention for today, something you want to manifest or achieve. Write it down and consider how to infuse it with purity and greatness.

Throughout the day, affirm this intention with confidence.

Day 6: It's In Your Hands, USE IT!
- **Affirmation:** "I hold the power to shape my destiny. I use my power wisely and purposefully."
- **Explanation:** Your life is in your hands. This affirmation reminds you of the incredible power you possess to influence the direction of your journey.
- **Anecdote:** Think of your power as a tool, like a sculptor's chisel. You can use it to shape your life into a masterpiece. The key is using it with intention.
- **Exercise:** Identify an area of your life where you feel you have the power to make a positive change. Set a specific goal for that area and plan how you will use your ability to achieve it.

Day 7: Everyone Cannot Go-Release and Receive
- **Affirmation:** "I release what no longer serves me. I make space to receive blessings and opportunities."
- **Explanation:** Sometimes, you must let go of what is holding you back to make room for new blessings

and opportunities. This affirmation encourages you to do just that.
- **Anecdote:** Imagine you're holding a bag of heavy rocks. You can't pick up new treasures with your hands full. By releasing the stones, you create space to receive something better.
- **Exercise:** Take an inventory of your life and identify something you're holding onto that no longer serves you—a bad habit, a negative belief, or a toxic relationship. Make a conscious effort to release it.

Day 8: Clean YOUR Windshields
- **Affirmation:** "I clear my vision for the future. Clarity and focus guide me on my journey."
- **Explanation:** Your vision for the future is like a windshield; it must be straightforward to navigate effectively. This affirmation encourages you to gain clarity and focus on your path.
- **Anecdote:** Think of your vision as a pair of glasses. You can see the world with precision when they're clean and clear. Clarity in your goals and aspirations is just as vital.

- **Exercise:** Take a few moments to meditate or visualize your ideal future. What does it look like? What steps can you take today to move closer to that vision?

Day 9: It's A Love Thing/Lifting You Higher

- **Affirmation:** "Love is at the core of my being. I lift myself and others higher through love."
- **Explanation:** Love is a powerful force for personal growth and positive change. This affirmation reminds you to nurture self-love and share love with others.
- **Anecdote:** Picture love as a flame within your heart. The more you feed it, the brighter it burns. This warmth can lift you higher and light the way for others.
- **Exercise:** Write a love letter to yourself. Acknowledge your strengths, beauty, and worthiness. Express genuine love and appreciation for who you are.

Day 10: YOUR Conversations: Expectations

- **Affirmation:** "My conversations are filled with positivity and high expectations. I create an empowering dialogue."

- **Explanation:** The conversations you have, both with others and with yourself, greatly influence your mindset. This affirmation encourages you to engage in empowering dialogues.
- **Anecdote:** Imagine your conversations as seeds planted in your mind. Positive conversations nurture the growth of empowering beliefs and high expectations.
- **Exercise:** Pay attention to your self-talk and interactions with others today. Whenever you catch negative or disempowering thoughts or conversations, consciously replace them with positive, empowering ones.

Day 11: No Trust, No Truth: Boss Up FINALLY TRUSTING YOURSELF

- **Affirmation:** "I trust myself completely. Trust is the foundation of my truth and authenticity."
- **Explanation:** Self-trust is the cornerstone of authenticity and living your truth. This affirmation reminds you to trust your instincts and inner wisdom.
- **Anecdote:** Consider trusting the solid ground upon which you stand. You may feel like you're on shaky

footing without trust in yourself. Trust provides stability.

- **Exercise:** Recall a time when you trusted your instincts, and it led to a positive outcome. Reflect on that experience and affirm your trust in yourself moving forward.

Day 12: A Moment In Time, Be Still

- **Affirmation:** "I find stillness in the present moment. In stillness, I discover clarity and inner peace."
- **Explanation:** Amid the busyness of life, finding moments of stillness is essential for clarity and inner peace. This affirmation invites you to embrace the present moment.
- **Anecdote:** Picture your mind as a pond, disturbed by ripples of thoughts and worries. Stillness is like calming those ripples, allowing you to see your reflection.
- **Exercise:** Dedicate at least ten minutes to sit quietly and focus on your breath. When your thoughts wander, gently guide your attention back to your breath. This practice can help you find stillness.

Day 13: The Covenant: Signed, Sealed, & Delivered

- **Affirmation:** "I honor the covenant of my purpose. My commitment is unwavering, and my purpose is fulfilled."
- **Explanation:** Your purpose is like a sacred covenant, and your commitment is the seal. This affirmation encourages you to remain dedicated to your life's purpose.
- **Anecdote:** Visualize your purpose as a path laid out before you. Each step you take is a commitment to fulfill that purpose. Your unwavering commitment keeps you on the way.
- **Exercise:** Write a personal mission statement encapsulating your purpose and commitment. Review it daily as a reminder of your unwavering dedication.

Day 14: Oil TOO Expensive, Time TOO Valuable

- **Affirmation:** "My time is precious and valuable. I use my time wisely to invest in my growth and purpose."
- **Explanation:** Time is a precious resource, and how you spend it dramatically impacts your journey.

This affirmation emphasizes the importance of using your time wisely.
- **Anecdote:** Consider time as currency; you can't get it back once spent. Investing your time in activities that nurture your growth and purpose is akin to investing in a valuable asset.
- **Exercise:** Create a weekly schedule that allocates dedicated time for activities that align with your growth and purpose. Track how you spend your time and make adjustments as needed.

Day 15: The Mountain Experiences, It Is Written
- **Affirmation:** "I embrace challenges as opportunities for growth. My experiences are written into the story of my life."
- **Explanation:** Challenges and obstacles are part of your journey, and this affirmation encourages you to view them as opportunities for growth.
- **Anecdote:** Picture your life as a book. The challenging chapters, like climbing mountains, are where the most profound growth occurs. These chapters make your story richer.
- **Exercise:** Reflect on a past challenge you faced and overcame. What did you learn from that experience,

and how did it shape you? Use this reflection as a reminder of your resilience.

Day 16: Own Your Power-Reassurance
- **Affirmation:** "I fully own my power and potential. Reassurance fuels my confidence and resilience."
- **Explanation:** Owning your power and potential is critical to success. This affirmation encourages you to take full ownership of your capabilities.
- **Anecdote:** Imagine your power and potential as a dormant fire within you. Owning it is like adding fuel to the fire. Reassurance is the spark that ignites it, fueling your confidence and resilience.
- **Exercise:** Make a list of your accomplishments and achievements. Review this list regularly to reassure yourself of your abilities and potential.

Day 17: A Chosen Essential Worker
- **Affirmation:** "I am an essential worker of divine purpose. My contributions are invaluable to the world."
- **Explanation:** You are not just a passive observer; you play an essential role in fulfilling your purpose. This affirmation reminds you of your significance.

- **Anecdote:** Think of your life as a grand production. You are a crucial actor in this play, and your contributions are essential to the storyline.
- **Exercise:** Identify one specific way your actions or contributions have positively impacted others or the world. Recognize the significance of your role.

Day 18: Living Your Kingdom Life Unapologetically
- **Affirmation:** "I live my kingdom life unapologetically. I am true to my purpose and values."
- **Explanation:** Living authentically according to your purpose and values is liberating. This affirmation encourages you to embrace your true self.
- **Anecdote:** Picture yourself as a unique puzzle piece that fits perfectly into the puzzle of life. By living authentically, you complete the larger picture with your distinct shape.
- **Exercise:** Write down your core values and principles. Reflect on how well you align your actions and decisions with these values.

Day 19: Anchored In Self-Care & Self-Love

- **Affirmation:** "I am anchored in self-care and self-love. Self-care nourishes my soul, and self-love empowers me."
- **Explanation:** Self-care and self-love are essential for maintaining balance and empowerment. This affirmation emphasizes their importance.
- **Anecdote:** Imagine self-care and self-love as the roots of a strong tree. When nourished, they provide stability and resilience, enabling you to weather life's storms.
- **Exercise:** Make a list of self-care activities that replenish your energy and self-love practices that boost your self-esteem. Commit to incorporating these into your routine.

Day 20: Serving The Nations Gratitude

- **Affirmation:** "I serve with gratitude and humility. My service enriches the lives of others and brings joy."
- **Explanation:** Service is a powerful way to make a positive impact. This affirmation encourages you to serve with a grateful and humble heart.

- **Anecdote:** Picture service as a bridge connecting you to others. Gratitude and humility are the sturdy pillars that support this bridge, ensuring it remains solid and beneficial.
- **Exercise:** Engage in service today, whether volunteering, helping a friend, or offering a kind gesture. Reflect on the joy and fulfillment it brings.

Day 21: Purpose, Not Performance

- **Affirmation:** "I focus on purpose, not performance. My fulfillment comes from aligning with my purpose."
- **Explanation:** Your journey isn't about impressing others or achieving external benchmarks. This affirmation reminds you that true fulfillment comes from aligning with your purpose.
- **Anecdote:** Imagine a race where the finish line represents your purpose. Instead of competing with others, focus on running your race and staying true to your path.
- **Exercise:** Reflect on a moment when you were genuinely aligned with your purpose, regardless of external recognition or performance. How did it feel? Use that memory as a guide for your journey ahead.

Conclusion

Your Journey to Greatness

Congratulations on completing the "Focusing 2 Finish 21 Day Affirmations" journey! Armed with faith and daily affirmations, you possess the tools to reshape your life, embrace your purpose, and impact future generations. Your journey to greatness is not only possible; it is inevitable. Remember that your words can shape your destiny as you focus on finishing strong. Embrace your greatness and create a legacy of inspiration.